Fact Finders®

EXTREME LIFE

ANIMALS WITH NO EYES

CAVE ADAPTATION

BY KELLY REGAN BARNHILL

Consultant:
Richard Borowsky, PhD
Department of Biology
New York University

Capstone
press®

Mankato, Minnesota

Fact Finders are published by Capstone Press,
151 Good Counsel Drive, P.O. Box 669, Mankato, Minnesota 56002.
www.capstonepress.com

Library of Congress Cataloging-in-Publication Data
Barnhill, Kelly Regan.
    Animals with no eyes : cave adaptation/ by Kelly Regan Barnhill.
    p. cm. — (Fact Finders. Extreme life)
    Summary: "Describes adaptations that occur in a cave environment, including general
adaptations and examples" — Provided by publisher.
    Includes bibliographical references.
    ISBN-13: 978-1-4296-1262-3 (hardcover)
    ISBN-10: 1-4296-1262-2 (hardcover)
    1. Cave animals — Adaptation — Juvenile literature. I. Title. II. Series.
QL117.B37 2008
591.75'84 — dc22   2007020896

Editorial Credits
Jennifer Besel, editor; Alison Thiele, designer; Linda Clavel, photo researcher,
    Danielle Ceminsky, cave zones illustrator

Photo Credits
Art Brown, 17; Corbis/DK Limited, 6 (middle); Corbis/Eric and David Hosking, 19; Corbis/
Lynda Richardson, 6 (right); Corbis/Sygma/Jean Becker, 28 (left); F.G. Howarth, 25; Getty
Images Inc./Jozsef Szentpeteri, 7; James P. Rowan, 8–9; Joseph J. Hobbs, 14; Nature Picture
Library/John Downer, 21; Peter Arnold/Matt Meadows, 11; Photo Researchers Inc./Francesco
Tomasinelli, 12–13; Shutterstock/Andy Heyward, 27 (background); Shutterstock/Domen
Lombergar, 4–5; Shutterstock/Helder Joaquim Soares de Almeida, 6 (background);
Shutterstock/Marek Szumlas, 27 (flashlight); Shutterstock/Peter Asprey, 6 (left); Shutterstock/
Piotr Sikora, 27 (rope); Stephen T. Samoray, 20; Visuals Unlimited/Ken Lucas, 10; Wind Cave
National Park, 28–29 (right); www.anotheca.com/Danté Fenolio, cover, 16, 22–23, 26;
www.glowworm.co.nz/Pete & Libby Chandler, 24

1 2 3 4 5 6 13 12 11 10 09 08

Table of Contents

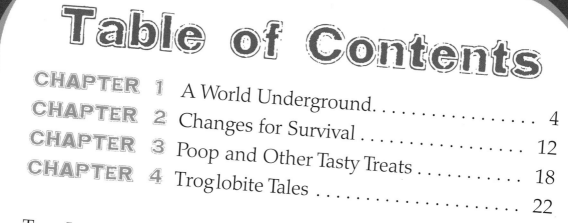

CHAPTER 1

A WORLD UNDERGROUND

Imagine you wake up one night, but instead of in your own bed, you find yourself in a cave. You're 300 feet (91 meters) under the surface of the earth. There is no light. None. You wiggle your fingers in front of your eyes like mad, but you can't see a thing. The air is chilly and damp, and you shiver in your pajamas. From far away, you hear water drip, drip, dripping onto the rock. A bat squeaks. Something small scurries nearby. And something cold and slimy has just brushed up against your bare foot!

Could you survive?

Without supplies, maps, and training, you probably couldn't survive.

adaptation: a change an animal or plant goes through to survive in its environment

The olm salamander lives underwater in some caves. The olm has no eyes or color. But it can live to be 100 years old!

Humans have developed **adaptations** to live above ground. Our eyes adjust to differences in light. We are good with tools and do well in groups. In caves, food is scarce and predators are everywhere. The creatures in caves have their own special adaptations that allow them to survive deep under the surface of the earth.

CAVE ZONES

ENTRANCE ZONE

TWILIGHT ZONE

DARK ZONE

Enter the Cave

When you walk into a cave, you'll notice that the world becomes cool and shadowy. You'll see some plants, like moss and ferns, that can grow with only a bit of light. This place is the entrance zone, the doorway to the world of the cave.

In the entrance zone, you'll find animals that move freely in and out of the cave. Bats, cave crickets, and even raccoons are animals that come and go.

cave cricket

These cave guests are called **trogloxenes**. Trogloxenes use caves for hibernation, for shelter during bad storms, or as a bedroom to get some shut-eye.

Trogloxenes make the perfect cave guests. They bring food! Lots and lots of food. They gather food on the surface and bring it back into the cave, where other cave animals help them eat it.

The Twilight Zone

If you walk a bit farther in, you'll find yourself in the twilight zone. A tiny amount of light still slips in on the cool, wet rocks. But the darkness is deep and growing. You might look around for something to eat. There are no more plants. There's just bat poop, fungus, and bacteria. Still hungry? I didn't think so.

Troglophiles, or "cave-lovers," usually live in the twilight zone of the cave. They love their cave, but from time to time they take a trip to the surface. The cool thing about troglophiles is that they can live all their lives in or out of the cave. Long-tailed salamanders, worms, and even some spiders are good examples of troglophiles.

troglophile: an animal that can spend all its life in a cave or can live outside a cave

Long-tailed salamanders thrive in the cool, dark twilight zone of some caves.

Deep in the Dark Zone

The deepest part of the cave is called the dark zone. It doesn't take long to get there. Just slip through one or two narrow passageways, and you'll find yourself in a world with no light at all.

The blind cave tetra couldn't live anywhere other than its home in the total darkness of a cave.

No eyes, no color. That's the life for this cave crayfish.

Deep in the dark zone, some amazing animals survive. These animals are called **troglobites**, or "cave-dwellers." Troglobites live in a world where eyes are useless and color doesn't matter. To survive, troglobites have adapted to the dark. In fact, they are so adapted to their cave environment that they would not be able to survive anywhere else.

CHAPTER 2

CHANGES FOR SURVIVAL

Change is good. You've heard people say that, right? When it comes to animals that survive in caves, change was very good. Many cave animals have relatives that live above ground. At some point, a few members of the family ended up in a cave. Not all the animals survived. But over time, some of the creatures' bodies changed in ways that kept them alive in the deep, dark cave.

Cave animal adaptations are crazy and cool, but they also serve a purpose. Adaptations aren't meant to make the animals pretty. They are meant to help animals stay alive. Let's take a look at some of the amazing ways cave creatures have adapted.

Even some millipedes have adapted to life deep in caves.

GROSS!

Many cave millipedes eat
rotting animal or plant pieces.

Belize land crab

No Eyes?

It's dark in a cave. Really dark. In a world of all black, eyes are useless. Troglobites have adapted to living without seeing. Most troglobites are blind. In fact, some cave creatures are born without any eyes at all. Why waste energy developing eyes if they won't help keep you alive?

INTERVIEW WITH A KENTUCKY CAVE SHRIMP

INTERVIEWER: Here we are in Mammoth Cave National Park and I've just run into the rare Kentucky cave shrimp. Hello!

SHRIMP: Hi! Welcome to the cave. I smelled you with my antennae. I thought you might be my supper.

INTERVIEWER: Uh, well, no. I was just wondering how you like life in the cave.

SHRIMP: Well, I've never lived anywhere else. But I like it just fine. I like walking on the bottom of the cave stream. And there's plenty of dead things to eat.

INTERVIEWER: I see that you don't have any eyes.

SHRIMP: Nope. Don't need 'em. Couldn't see anyway. It's so dark in here. But I better move on. Like I said, I'm looking for supper.

Ghostly Creatures

Another adaptation has to do with color — or the lack of it. Unlike animals above ground, troglobites don't need camouflage. Their predators probably don't have eyes to see them anyway. Many cave animals have lost their markings and their bodies have turned a ghostly white.

cave crayfish

Seeing without Eyes

Although they're blind, troglobites aren't helpless. Actually, these animals use other senses to make up for not being able to see. They use smell, taste, and touch to know where they are going and if another animal is coming. Many troglobites have really long legs or antennae to feel their way around.

Cave fish use their vibration sensors to survive in underwater caves or in cave pools.

Uncommon Sense

Some troglobites have developed another way to know what's going on around them. These animals have a sense organ on their bodies that picks up vibrations or changes in pressure. This adaptation is super handy. It allows animals to know where rocks or bumps are or where other creatures are moving.

POOP AND OTHER TASTY TREATS

CHAPTER 3

Deep underground, a troglobite is waking up from a short nap. He's hungry. Really, really hungry. Where on earth is this poor blind creature going to get its food?

Enter the bat.

Most caves are open systems. That means that they have an entrance to the outside world. In open system caves, bats help the rest of the animals by keeping out insects that could carry disease. But most importantly, they produce a rich food source in the form of their **guano**.

guano: bat poop

GROSS!

Bat guano has lots of protein and minerals. Some scientists say if we could sanitize it, guano would be a great food for people too.

BAT POOP SURPRISE!

Mealtime blahs got your family down? Spice things up a bit with Bat Poop Surprise! Little cave creatures will love the crunchy cave fish crust with a juicy poop center!

INGREDIENTS: Four cave fish, four servings guano

INSTRUCTIONS:

1. After successfully catching the cave fish, remove the heads.
2. Stuff the bodies with a generous helping of guano.
3. Just for fun, put the heads back on.
4. Serve on a flat rock. Enjoy!

Delicious Poop

Bats' bodies only absorb a small amount of the nutrients in their food. That means when a bat eats a fly, part of the fly will come out in the bat's poop. And poop filled with flies and other undigested food is really tasty to a troglobite.

GROSS!

Bats often rest in the same spot in a cave. Their poop stacks up beneath them, making piles that can get several feet high.

Sacred Cenote sinkhole in Mexico

Sinking Food

Poop can get boring, even for a troglobite. What else is yummy? Fungus! Dead animals!

Many caves are connected to the outside through **sinkholes**. Water collects in sinkholes, along with leaves, grasses, and dead animals. All this material rots, allowing fungus and bacteria to grow. As water drains from the sinkholes into the cave, the dead material, fungus, and bacteria come with it. All of this combines into a thick, stinky slop that's a feast for a hungry troglobite.

CHAPTER 4

TROGLOBITE TALES

Caves are home to hundreds of animals. But some of the most amazing cave creatures are the troglobites. Let's take a look at a few deep cave creatures to see how they use adaptations to stay alive.

Ghost Lizards

Grotto salamanders, also known as "ghost lizards," are white or pale pink with light orange stripes on their tails and feet. These creatures are born with both gills and eyes. But as they become adults, three things happen. First, they grow smaller, not bigger. Second, their eyes stop working and are slowly sucked back into their bodies. Third, their gills close up, and they begin to breathe through their skin. Amazing adaptations, don't you think?

GROSS!

Some troglobites will eat members of their own species. That would be like you eating your brother!

Can you imagine growing smaller and having your eyes sucked back into your body like this grotto salamander? Crazy!

Glowworms

If you or I visited a cave, we would need flashlights. But some animals have their own built-in flashlights. In New Zealand's Waitomo Cave, glowworms light up to lure bugs into their fishing lines (or single-threaded webs). No batteries needed!

The glowworms hang down their sticky threads to catch a tasty treat.

No-Eyed Big-Eyed Spider

The no-eyed big-eyed spider lives only in the warm, humid caves in Kauai, one of the Hawaiian islands. Long ago, the ancestors of the no-eyed big-eyed spider wandered into the caves. They found food. They avoided predators. They survived.

Over time, they changed. Their eyes got smaller until finally they disappeared. They used sensors in their legs to find food. The darkness became a tool for hunting and for hiding. And now the no-eyed big-eyed spider depends on the protection of the cave to survive.

Blind Salamander

The Georgia blind salamander is one of the rarest creatures in America. These salamanders have no eyes. They have just two black dots marking the place where their ancestors once had eyes. They live in pools of water deep inside caves.

Georgia blind salamanders use motion sensors on their bodies to know if something is nearby. When they are in danger, they swim in a spiral toward the top of the water. When they get to the surface, they lie still and float slowly back down. Playing dead is a great way for the salamander to "see" another day.

ADAPTATION ADVENTURE

Today, you are the most famous cave biologist in the world. You are down in the deep, deep, deep earth. You have your trusty flashlight, your best ropes, your scientific instruments, and your sense of adventure. And you've just discovered a brand new creature!

What adaptations does this creature have to survive? What does it eat? How does it find food? Draw a picture of the creature and write a paragraph describing its special adaptations and how it survives in the deep, dark cave.

Amazing Adaptation

Adaptations don't happen overnight. It takes many, many years for animals to develop adaptations like the ones these eyeless, colorless, bat-poop-eating creatures have. Adaptations are amazing, but they are also necessary for survival.

TRUE LIVES OF SCIENTISTS

Finding troglobites isn't easy. Cave scientists can't just walk into a cave and spot them sitting on a rock, waiting for someone to take their picture. Cave scientists have to travel to the deepest, darkest parts of the cave to find the creatures with no eyes.

Ready, Set, Crawl

So how do they get down into the dark cave areas? Well, first they grab their gear: helmets, warm clothing, knee pads, cameras, and of course, lights. Oh, and for the deepest caves, they'll need ropes and equipment to lower themselves down hundreds of feet to the bottom of deep pits.

While hauling all this gear, scientists wiggle and crawl through wet, muddy, and narrow cave passageways. It can take hours or even days to reach the troglobites' home. And remember, once the scientists finish their research, they still have to wiggle and crawl their way back out.

Concerned Cavers

When they're not exploring caves, cave scientists work to educate others about how to protect troglobites from pollution, poison, and disturbance. Sometimes cave scientists are the only thing protecting cave creatures from certain extinction. They're kind of like superheroes for troglobites. How cool is that?

GLOSSARY

ADAPTATION (ad-ap-TAY-shuhn) — a change that a living thing goes through to fit in better with its environment

CAMOUFLAGE (KAM-uh-flahzh) — coloring or covering that makes animals, people, and objects look like their surroundings

GUANO (GWAH-noh) — animal droppings

PREDATOR (PRED-uh-tur) — an animal that hunts other animals for food

SINKHOLE (SINGK-hohl) — a hollow place in the ground where drainage collects

TROGLOBITE (TRAWG-loh-bite) — an animal that can only survive in a cave environment

TROGLOPHILE (TRAWG-loh-file) — an animal that can live all its life either inside or outside a cave

TROGLOXENE (TRAWG-loh-zeen) — an animal that spends part of its life in a cave, but must leave the cave to survive

INTERNET SITES

FactHound offers a safe, fun way to find Internet sites related to this book. All of the sites on FactHound have been researched by our staff.

Here's how:

1. Visit *www.facthound.com*

2. Choose your grade level.

3. Type in this book ID **1429612622** for age-appropriate sites. You may also browse subjects by clicking on letters, or by clicking on pictures and words.

4. Click on the **Fetch It** button.

FactHound will fetch the best sites for you!

READ MORE

Allman, Toney. *Life in a Cave*. Ecosystems. Detroit: KidHaven Press, 2005.

Banting, Erinn. *Caves*. Biomes. New York: Weigl, 2006.

Lynette, Rachel. *Caves*. Wonders of the World. Detroit: KidHaven Press, 2005.

INDEX